DRAWS CRITICISM

Published by

Chatsworth Press
29 Chatsworth Avenue
Glyndon, Maryland
21071
www.kaltoons.com

Design

Glenn Dellon / Dellon Design
529 North Charles Street 101
Baltimore, Maryland
21201
gdellon@comcast.net

Printing

Ridge Printing
4627 Ridge Road
Baltimore, Maryland
21236
P 410 668 4780 / **F** 410 668 0469

All cartoons in this book are from **The Baltimore Sun, The Economist,** and **The Digger.**
©1988, 1989, 1992, 1997, 1999, 2000, 2001, 2002, 2003, 2004, 2005, 2006

ISBN — 1-4243-0052-5
Library of Congress Control Number: 2006923021

Kevin Kallaugher's cartoons are distributed exclusively by

CartoonArts International / The New York Times Syndicate
27520 Hawthorne Boulevard
Suite 174
Rolling Hills Estates, California
90274
P 310 265 8787 / www.cartoonweb.com

KAI
DRAWS CRITICISM

Other books by Kevin Kallaugher

Kal Draws The Line
The Baltimore Sun, 2000

Kal Draws A Crowd
Woodholme House, 1997

Kaltoons
Chatsworth Press, 1992

Drawn from the Economist
The Economist Publications, 1988

Table of Contents

These are trying times for political cartoonists.

The recent publication in Denmark of irreverent cartoons depicting the prophet Mohammed sparked deadly protests around the globe. The 12 Danish artists who drew the cartoons now live in fear as Osama Bin Laden has called for their execution. Elsewhere, in Belarus, Zimbabwe, and Iran, political cartoonists fear violent retribution from government thugs because of their art.

Here in America, editorial cartoonists are also under pressure. The cartoonists are not under physical threat but their proud profession is slowly dying. The great American cartoon once wielded the power to topple politicians. Now, newspaper owners regard it as an expendable artifact. In recent decades the number of professional cartoonists in America has been cut in half to just over 100. Prominent newspapers like the New York Times, Wall Street Journal and The Los Angeles Times do not employ a staff political cartoonist. Other newspapers, in cost cutting frenzies, are eliminating cartoonists from their payrolls. With circulation and advertising numbers declining, desperate publishers and accountants are looking for answers to their budget woes. The cartoonist looks an easy target for their budget ax. With every salaried position lost, newspapers, their readers and the cartoonist community become poorer as a result.

Yet despite these tales of woe, there is hope for the beleaguered cartoonist.

Up to now the plight of the political cartoon has been tied the plight of newspapers. But today newspaper readers are increasingly turning to the Internet as a source for news and information. As Americans move from the printed page to the computer screen the political cartoonist will move with them. Cartoonists will find a way to use the web as a new medium for their satirical commentary.

Unlike the traditional newspaper cartoon that had for long employed the static tools of print – pens, crayons and cross hatching – the new Internet cartoons will move. Advancing computer technology will allow cartoonists to create animated cartoons in increasingly shorter time spans. New styles and approaches to political cartooning will grow out of the new tools available. New venues for animated political satire on the web, television and cable will appear. The political cartoon is poised for a renaissance.

I could write a book about the future of cartooning. This book however is about the past. It is a collection of "Old School" cartoons from what may soon be a bygone era. An era of black and white images rendered in cross-hatching with crow quill nibs dipped in India ink.

Don't get me wrong. I am deeply fond of the traditional political cartoon. As much as I am excited about the challenges of the Internet age, I love the directness and simplicity of ink on paper. I much prefer the imperfection of a scratchy pen line to the clarity of clean computer rendering.

You will find in this book five years worth of my favorite scratchy lines. The collection includes cartoons from **The Economist** magazine and **The Baltimore Sun** that comment on a wide range of important issues and historic events including the hotly contested US election of 2000, the attacks of September 11, and the War in Iraq.

I am very proud of these cartoons. For me, they represent a milestone. I have struggled for three decades to master the craft of the newspaper political cartoon. Looking at the enclosed collection of my recent work I feel encouraged that I may be close to attaining that goal.

But the future of newspaper cartoons is dimming. Recognizing that reality, I am one of those political cartoonists looking to embrace the Internet and the moving image as a future source of satire. I plan to continue practicing and perfecting the scratchy line while simultaneously exploring the magic of computer rendering and animation.

Where this new form of satire will take me is, at present, unknown. What is known is the newspapers' relevance in our society is dwindling along with it the future of the conventional newspaper political cartoon.

Yes, these are trying times for political cartoonists.

I'm trying something new.

~Kevin Kallaugher

F

KAL
DRAWS CRITICISM

CHAPTER ONE

CAMPAIGNS

The election of the president by public vote is the defining act of our democracy. The campaign leading up to this election, however, is anything but dignified. It is tedious and getting longer, more polemic and shriller, with all the gravitas of a sitcom.

The Baltimore Sun
09 25 2005

The Baltimore Sun
07 27 2000

The Governor of Texas George W. Bush chose long-time family friend Dick Cheney as his running mate.

The Economist
06 03 2000

Green Party candidate Ralph Nader siphoned off valuable votes from Democratic Party nominee Al Gore.

The Baltimore Sun
11 09 2000

The Economist

03 22 2001

National politics became more bitter, partisan, and polarized in the months and years after the 2000 election.

The Baltimore Sun
11 09 2002

The 2002 mid-term elections
humbled the Democrats.

The Baltimore Sun

01 06 2004

The former Vermont
Governor Howard Dean was
an early favorite for the
Democratic nomination.

The Economist
03 05 2004
Within weeks of the New Hampshire primary, Bush and Kerry had garnered their respective party's nominations.

The Baltimore Sun
10 21 2004

The Economist

08 05 2004

The candidates dedicated a disproportionate amount of resources to a handful of key, disputed states.

SWING STATES · PLEASE PLAY NICELY

The Baltimore Sun
09 08 2004

The 2004 presidential campaign was the most expensive and vitriolic in memory.

The Baltimore Sun
11 02 2004

The Baltimore Sun
11 04 2004

Republicans strengthened
their hold on the White
House and Congress.

KEVIN KALLAUGHER

KAL

DRAWS CRITICISM

CHAPTER TWO

2

AMERICA AT HOME

The campaign is over. Now we have to live with the results as promises are put into action ... or not. Despite the government's good intentions, many problems remain in American society. Drawing attention to these problems has long been the mission of the editorial cartoonist.

The Baltimore Sun
08 03 2003

The Baltimore Sun
02 06 2001

Aggressive tax cuts were a high economic priority for the President.

The Economist
10 25 2004

Bill Clinton left George W.
Bush an ample budget
surplus. It didn't last long.

The Baltimore Sun

03 20 2001

The corrupting influence of money continued to be felt in Washington. A few brave souls dared to challenge it.

The Baltimore Sun
07 03 2005

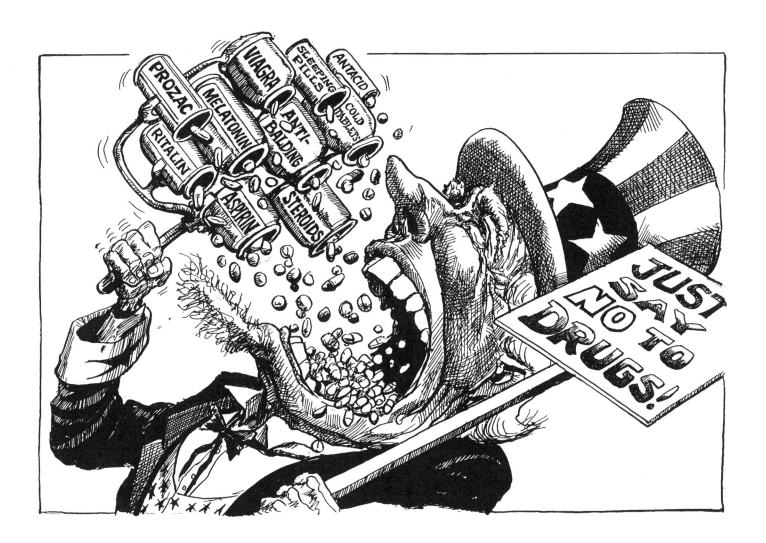

The Baltimore Sun

06 07 2005

The Federal Government strictly enforced the ban on medical marijuana.

The Baltimore Sun
07 15 2004

The Baltimore Sun

09 27 2005

In several states, citizens tried to reintroduce creationism into school curriculums under the pseudonym of intelligent design.

The Baltimore Sun
10 09 2003

A political novice, Arnold Schwarzenegger, was elected governor of California.

The Baltimore Sun
07 03 2005

Filling vacancies in the
Supreme Court ignited the
Nation's passions.

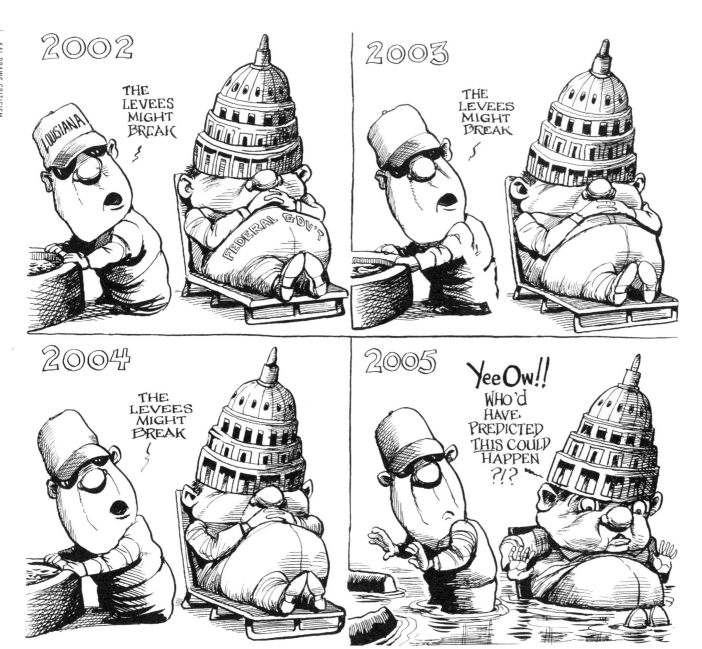

The Baltimore Sun

09 04 2005

No one was prepared for the devastating power of Hurricane Katrina.

The Baltimore Sun
09 07 2005

The Baltimore Sun
04 22 2005

The Baltimore Sun
07 28 2005

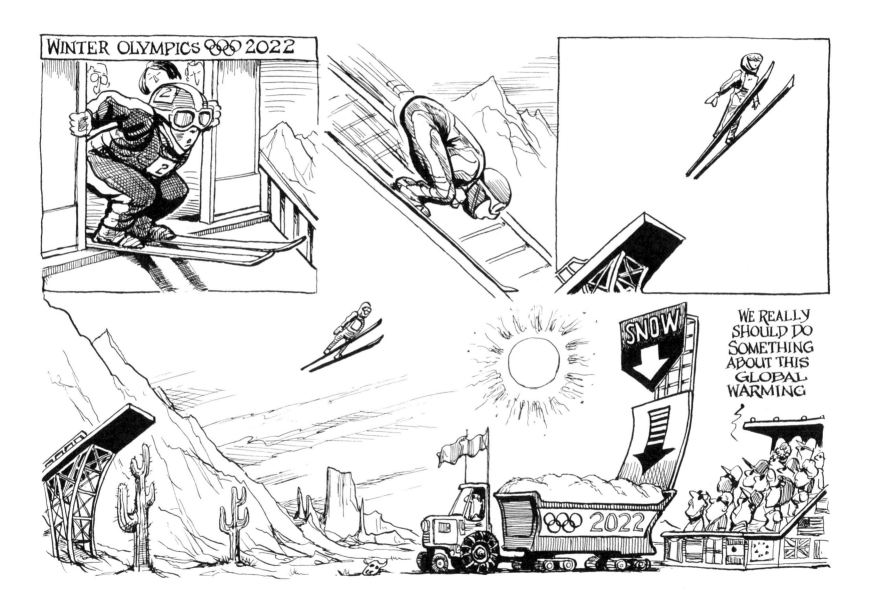

The Baltimore Sun
06 06 2000

KAL DRAWS CRITICISM

CHAPTER THREE

NOT JUST FOR SUNDAY

As a kid I looked forward to reading Doonesbury in color on the Sunday comic pages. It was exciting watching the daily black and white cartoons explode with color on the weekend. As a professional, I've had the opportunity to dabble with this vibrant medium. Throughout the years, I've drawn over 100 covers for **The Economist.** Here are some of my favorite color cartoons.

The Economist
04 22 2004
11 11 2003
01 06 2005
11 01 2001

Clockwise from top left.

The Economist
01 18 1997
11 04 1989
08 16 2003

The Digger
01 01 1988

Clockwise from top left.

The Economist

05 11 2005

People looked on nervously as Bush performed on the world stage.

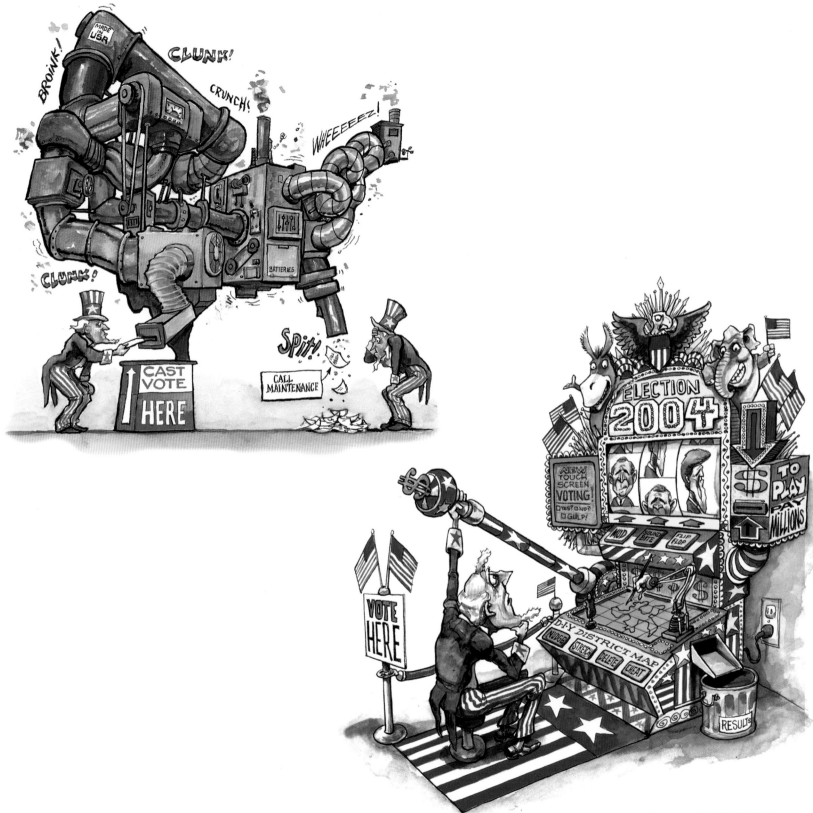

OPPOSITE
The Economist
01 20 2001
10 04 2004

THIS PAGE
The Economist
01 20 2001

The fiasco in Florida high-lighted the inadequacies in the American electoral process.

The Economist
10 04 2004

The Economist
10 26 2005

Hurricanes damaged the
President's credibility.

OPPOSITE

The Economist

07 06 2005

The Supreme Court was a political battleground.

THIS PAGE

The Economist

02 17 2006

12 05 2002

05 26 2005

01 12 2006

02 17 2006

03 27 2003

02 15 2006

05 20 2004

07 16 2005

Top to bottom, left to right.

The Economist
12 04 2002

Kim Jong-il, leader of
North Korea, gave the world
a nuclear headache.

The Economist
02 17 2006

Oilaholics.

The Economist
01 20 2001

The Baltimore Sun
09 16 2001

President Clinton proved to
be more than two-faced.

KEVIN KALLAUGHER

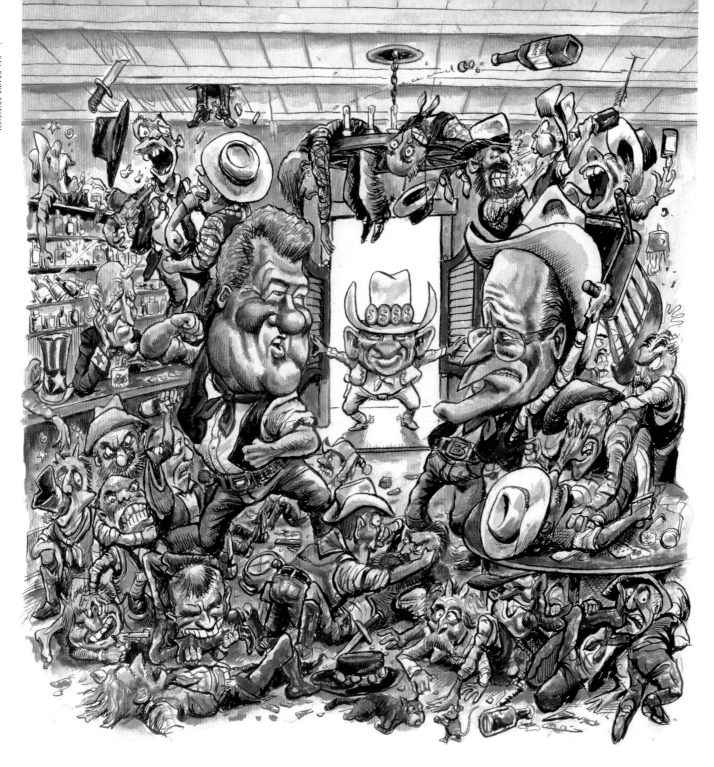

The Economist
1992

Billionaire Ross Perot entered the campaign as an independent candidate.

The Baltimore Sun

11 07 2001

The end of the Cold War changed the dynamics between the United States and Russia.

I WALK the LINE

The Washington Post
02 05 2006

KAL

DRAWS CRITICISM

ISLAMIC
TERRORISTS

CHAPTER FOUR

4

NINE ELEVEN

The months following the attacks of September 11, 2001 were full of pain and poignancy for Americans. The heightened awareness, sensitivity, and anxiety of the country made it a challenging time to be a cartoonist.

The Baltimore Sun
09 13 2001

The Baltimore Sun
09 18 2001

The Economist
09 19 2001

The Baltimore Sun
11 11 2001

The Baltimore Sun
09 27 2001

The Baltimore Sun
11 26 2001

The Baltimore Sun

12 09 2001

Attorney General John Ashcroft introduced the controversial Patriot Act. He was quick to condemn those who opposed his policies.

The Baltimore Sun

09 30 2001

Pennsylvania Governor Tom
Ridge was named the first
director of the new Homeland
Security Department.

The Economist
10 24 2001
The Taliban government in Afghanistan became the first target in the War on Terror.

The Baltimore Sun

12 08 2001

The West soon discovered
that Afghanistan was a
unified country in name only.

The Baltimore Sun
11 15 2001

As coalition forces advanced, many Afghanis chose to shed the beards associated with the authoritarian Taliban regime.

The Baltimore Sun

01 15 2002

The most powerful man on the planet nearly choked to death on a pretzel.

KAV

DRAWS CRITICISM

5

A WORLD IN TURMOIL

The U.S. government went on the offensive in the War on Terror, first in Afghanistan and then in Iraq. Initially, the vast majority of the American public was in favor of going to war. But as the epicenter of the war moved from Kabul to Baghdad, things started getting ugly.

The Baltimore Sun
11 11 2001

The Baltimore Sun
08 10 2002

The Bush administration focused intently on Saddam Hussein's Iraq.

The Economist
06 17 2004

The Baltimore Sun

02 16 2003

The administration wrongly believed that Iraq would quickly recover from a traumatic invasion.

The Economist

04 03 2002

Tony Blair, prime minister of
Great Britain, had a policy
toward Saddam Hussein that
was difficult to distinguish
from that of the U.S. President.

The Baltimore Sun
09 08 2002

GOING IN
IS THE
EASY PART...

IRAQ

AFGHANISTAN

The Baltimore Sun
04 06 2002

THE PRESIDENT ADDRESSES THE ARAB WORLD

IS THERE A SPIN DOCTOR IN THE HOUSE?

USA

The Baltimore Sun
05 07 2004

The video footage and photographs of Iraqi prisoners abused in U.S. custody at the Abu Ghraib prison shocked the world.

The Baltimore Sun

05 11 2004

Secretary of Defense Donald Rumsfeld was a central figure in the formulation of U.S. policy towards Iraq.

The Baltimore Sun
02 17 2004

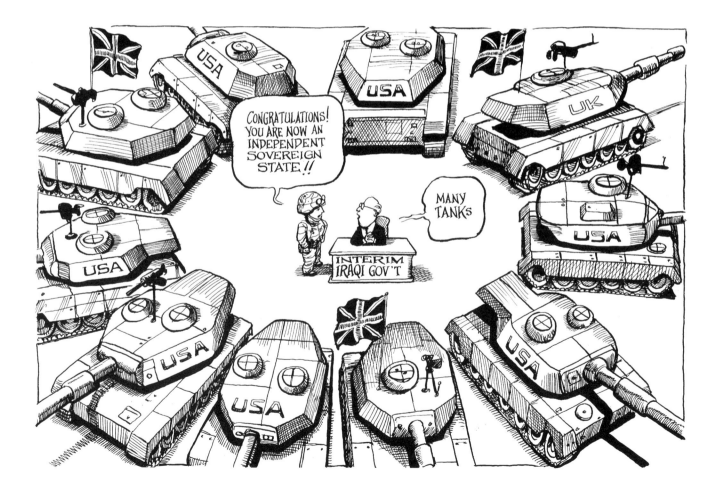

The Baltimore Sun
01 31 2004

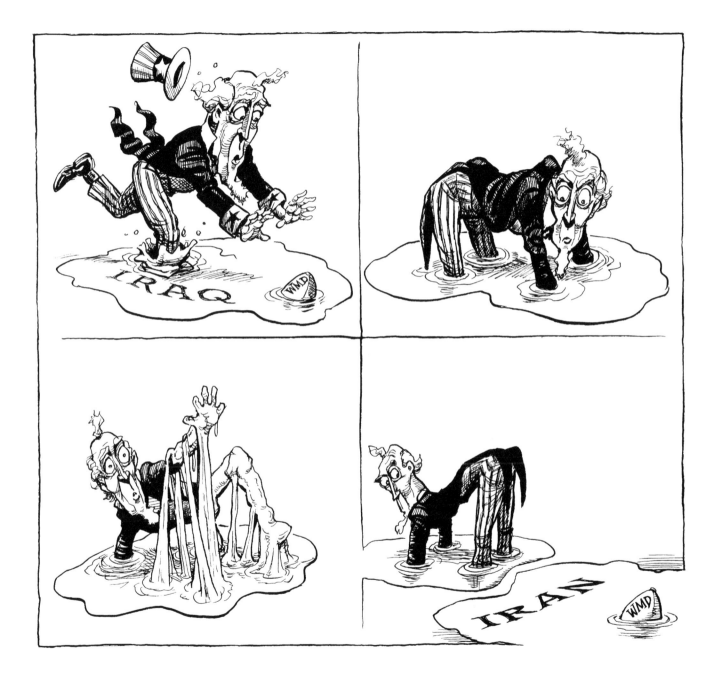

The Economist

07 28 2004

The government of
Iran defied the world and
enriched uranium.

The Economist

10 24 2002

Kim Jong-il of North Korea
got attention but no respect.

The Baltimore Sun
02 13 2005

The Economist
06 03 2005

The Economist

12 09 2004

The newly elected democratic government in Afghanistan set to work.

The Baltimore Sun
07 08 2001

Late Serbian leader Slobodan Milosevic was accused of war crimes in the Balkan conflict of the late 1990s.

The Economist

10 31 2002

Vladimir Putin's Russia struggled to quash the bloody insurgency in the former Russian republic of Chechnya.

The Economist
03 17 2005

The Baltimore Sun

01 11 2005

Mahmoud Abbas
replaced Yasser Arafat
as the President of
the Palestinian Authority.

The Baltimore Sun
02 10 2005

The Economist

09 23 2004

The world was unable to stop
yet another genocide,
this time in southern Sudan.

The Baltimore Sun
08 02 2005

In a controversial decision, President Bush appointed a vocal critic of the United Nations, John Bolton, to be U.S. Ambassador to the U.N.

The Baltimore Sun
03 20 2005

The Baltimore Sun
02 19 2002

CHAPTER SIX

KAL'S FAVORITES

I really like these cartoons. Some are funny, some are really well drawn, and some just didn't fit anywhere else in the book. It's a mish-mashed hodge-podge collection of my favorites. Nothing is safe as sports, culture, the environment, and even the Easter bunny get their licks.

The Baltimore Sun
10 04 1992

Texas billionaire Ross Perot made his presence felt in the 1992 presidential election.

The Baltimore Sun
06 02 2005

The Baltimore Sun
04 18 2004

The bipartisan 9-11 commission asked hard questions and made tough recommendations to the government.

The Baltimore Sun
05 27 2004

The Baltimore Sun
1989

As population exploded in the mid-Atlantic, the Chesapeake Bay's ecosystem came under siege.

The Economist
04 01 2004

The Economist
04 07 2005

Drivers became increasingly
frustrated as gas prices
lurched skyward.

The Baltimore Sun

03 17 2005

Major League Baseball
was tainted by allegations
of the use of
performance-enhancing
drugs by star players.

The Baltimore Sun
01 04 2004

Mad cow disease was a serious concern to both beef suppliers and consumers.

The Baltimore Sun
10 11 2005

The Baltimore Sun
06 08 2003

The Baltimore Sun
11 28 1999

The Baltimore Sun

01 13 2006

This was KAL's last cartoon
in The Baltimore Sun.

The cartoonist and author thanks **The Economist** magazine and **The Baltimore Sun** for their support in this book project. A particular thanks goes to Bill Emmott and Penny Garrett at The Economist for years of patience and encouragement.

Thanks, too, goes to Dianne Donovan and Will Englund at The Sun for giving me the freedom and independence required to excel at this unique craft.

The author would like to gratefully acknowledge Leeds Hackett without whose financial advice, guidance and support this book would not have been realized.

Finally, thanks to Glenn Dellon, designer of the book. It has been a source of great pride for me to see my one time high school intern blossom into a talented professional.

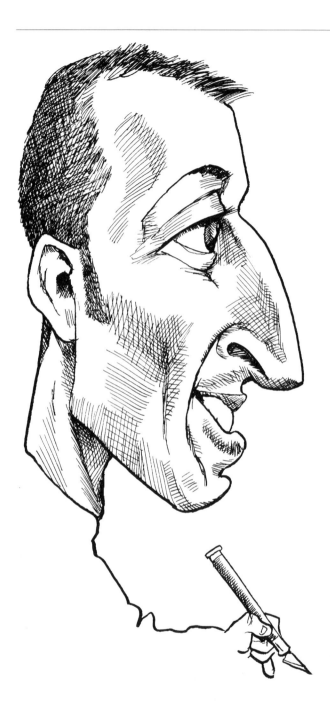

Glenn is the founder and creative principal of Dellon Design, an multidisciplinary studio specializing in strategy and brand. A native of Baltimore, he attended The Park School and graduated from Tufts University with degrees in Art History, Architectural History, and Fine Art. Immediately after college, he earned a graduate certificate in Graphic Design from The Maryland Institute College of Art as well as a Masters degree in Publication Design from the University of Baltimore.

A long time ago, Glenn worked with Kevin KAL Kallaugher for his Senior Project at Park. During this stretch as "Intern Boy," he learned quite a bit about about cartoons, art, politics, publications, and organizing ten years worth of photographs into a convenient filing system. For Glenn, a burgeoning cartoonist at the time, it was an unbelievable experience with none of the bitter aftertaste commonly associated with school. The opportunity to design this very book for KAL all these years later was even more improbable. Thus, he has recently (relative to the printing of this book) claimed the glass to be half full.

These days (relative to the printing of this book), Glenn is really into squirrels, light blue, and kofta challow from the Helmand restaurant located just up the street from his Mt. Vernon office.

INTERN BOY BY GLENN DELLON
CIRCA 1995

After graduating from Harvard University in 1977, Kevin Kallaugher decided against pursuing a career on Wall Street and instead embarked on a bicycle tour of the British Isles. The tour finished, but he stayed in the U.K., joining the Brighton Basketball Club as a player and coach. When the club hit financial difficulties, KAL drew caricatures of tourists in Trafalgar Square and on Brighton Pier. In March 1978, when he was down to his last pair of socks, The Economist magazine recruited him to become the first resident cartoonist in their 145-year history. Kevin spent the next 10 years working in London as a cartoonist for such publications as The Observer, The Sunday Telegraph, Today, and The Mail on Sunday. Twenty-eight years later, he is still the editorial cartoonist for The Economist. KAL returned to the United States in 1988 to join The Baltimore Sun as its editorial cartoonist. Over the course of 17 years, he drew over 4,000 cartoons for the Sun. KAL's association with the Sun ended in 2005.

KAL has been recognized internationally as a cartoonist of rare verve and talent. Among many honors, in 1982 he became Feature Cartoonist of the Year, a title bestowed upon him by the Cartoonist Club of Great Britain. In 1996, he received the Grafica Internazionale Award at the International Festival of Satire in Pisa, Italy. In 1999, 2002, and 2005, he was the recipient of the Thomas Nast award, presented by the Overseas Press Club of America. In 2004, he was awarded the "Gillray Goblet" for cartoon of the year, presented by the Political Cartoon Society of Great Britain. In 1999, The World Encyclopedia of Cartoons said of KAL: "Commanding a masterful style, Kallaugher stands among the premier caricaturists of the century."

KAL has had exhibitions in London, New York, Washington, D.C., and Baltimore. In the summer of 2006, the Walters Art Museum assembled a major KAL retrospective titled "Mightier than the Sword; the Satirical Pen of KAL" featuring over 200 examples of his work.

KAL is a past president of the Association of American Editorial Cartoonists and Cartoonists Rights Network. KAL continues to live in Baltimore, play basketball, and fly fish for trout on the Gunpowder River.

KAL

DRAWS CRITICISM